RACE, CLASS, AND THE POSTINDUS

SUNY series, The New Inequalities
A. Gary Dworkin, Editor

RACE,
CLASS,
AND THE
POSTINDUSTRIAL CITY

William Julius Wilson and the Promise of Sociology

FRANK HAROLD WILSON

State University of New York Press

Photograph of William Julius Wilson courtesy of the University of Chicago,
University News Office.

The author thanks the publishers of material used in this book: *The Bridge Over the Racial Divide: Rising Inequality and Coalition Politics.* By William Julius Wilson. Copyright © 1999. The Regents of the University of California. *When Work Disappears* by William Julius Wilson © 1996 by William Julius Wilson. Alfred A. Knopf, a division of Random House, Inc. William Julius Wilson, "Academic Controversy and Intellectual Growth." In *Sociological Lives: Social Change and the Life Course.* Vol. 2:81. Edited by Matilda White Riley. Copyright © 1988. Sage Publications, Inc. *The Truly Disadvantaged* by William Julius Wilson, Copyright © 1987. University of Chicago Press. *The Declining Significance of Race* by William Julius Wilson, Copyright © 1978. University of Chicago Press.

Published by
State University of New York Press, Albany

© 2004 State University of New York

For information, address State University of New York Press,
90 State Street, Suite 700, Albany, NY 12207

Production by Judith Block
Marketing by Jennifer Giovani and Susan Petrie

Library of Congress Cataloging-in-Publication Data

Wilson, Frank Harold.
    Race, class, and the postindustrial city : William Julius Wilson and the promise of sociology / Frank Harold Wilson.
        p. cm. — (SUNY series, the new inequalities)
    Includes bibliographical references and index.
    ISBN 0-7914-6015-0 (alk. paper) — ISBN 0-7914-6016-9 (pbk : alk. paper)
        1. Wilson, William J., 1935– 2. African American sociologists—Biography.
    3. Sociology, Urban—United States. 4. African Americans—Social conditions.
    5. African Americans—Economic conditions. 6. Urban poor—United States.
    7. Inner cities—United States. 8. United States—Race relations. 9. United
    States—Social policy. I. Title. II. Series.

HM479.W55 W55 2004
301'.0973—dc21
                                                            2003052616

CONTENTS

v

PREFACE

This book examines the intersection of race relations, social class, and urban problems in the scholarship of the sociologist, William Julius Wilson. Wilson, who currently is Lewis P. and Linda L. Geyser university professor at Harvard University, is a distinguished and nationally visible scholar who has become widely recognized in both academic and public policy circles. In a *Washington Post* article he was described as the "most influential sociologist of his generation" (Abramowitz 1991), and *Time* magazine in 1996 named him as one of America's twenty-five most influential Americans. Wilson's sociological writings are primarily concerned with analyzing questions of race relations using sociohistorical and theoretical perspectives. He is best known for the contemporary classics *The Declining Significance of Race* (1978), *The Truly Disadvantaged* (1987), and *When Work Disappears* (1996), where he has refocused recent public debates and research on poverty in general and the urban underclass specifically. His more recent scholarship and commentaries combine these interests with policy concerns focused on the inner-city poor and jobless.

I initially began writing this book as an article which attempted to critically appraise the theoretical and research controversies of class and race which were symbolized and influenced by *The Declining Significance of Race* and *The Truly Disadvantaged*. Early on, it became clear that an article would be insufficient to treat Wilson's scholarship in its complexity and many-layered meanings. There appeared to me to be many more dimensions of meaning and complexity in his scholarship than was coming across in the sociological controversies. A search for truth and meaning has helped guide this study.

Contained in Wilson's theoretical construction of social reality is a complexity of analysis that is frequently not understood or appreciated by his defenders and critics. This complexity partly grows out of his sociological imagination, which combines formal and pragmatic aims with a holistic analysis of post-World War II macrosociological changes such as industrialization, the growth of the government and public policies, urbanization, and changes among ethnic and racial groups that intersect with social-class conflicts. The holistic perspective used by Wilson is an exercise of theoretical research combining both normative and empirical approaches of sociological theory. The analyses in Wilson's scholarship synthesize and address a range of sociological, political, and cultural discourses that extend from the left to the right.

At the same time, there are contained in the criticisms of Wilson's analyses of class and race important voices which were generally neglected, distanced, discredited, and invalidated in mainstream discussions and publications. Aldon Morris notes in the controversy surrounding *The Declining Significance of Race* that while liberal academics largely portrayed Wilson as dispassionate, courageous, and radical, his Black critics were usually dismissed as overreactionary and emotional (Morris 1996, 312). It is instructive that many of the independent and critical commentaries by Black and White scholars based on philosophical, theoretical, and historical analyses and social science research evidence were "fenced out" of mainstream sociological journals. These are the invisible "voices behind the veil" which will enter the continuing and unresolved controversies of race and class. Among these invisible voices are prophetic voices.

Alongside the focus on race and class, Wilson's sociology is importantly informed by urban sociology; he has in turn helped influence research on urban questions through his framing of macrosociological models of society, numerous concepts, and hypotheses. It is instructive that Wilson's interests in race relations in the city coincide with his years at the University of Chicago and appear largely absent in his scholarship before this time. In fact, it is through the context of the Chicago School that he begins examining the significance of the Black urban experience. It should be mentioned at the outset that while Wilson does not appear to be consciously entertaining the development of a model or theory of Blacks in cities. In many respects, this theory of Blacks in cities appears more a serendipitous concern. Within public-policy circles, Wilson has become a leading urban expert. His appropriation and treatment of numerous concepts, models, hypotheses, and generalizations of race, class, and postindustrial society pull his work in the direction of urban sociological theory.

The intersection of race, class, and the city has long interested sociologists. Nearly one hundred years ago, W. E. B. Du Bois pioneered the first systematic study of organized life in an urban community in *The Philadelphia Negro: A Social Study* (1899) and established the Sociological Laboratory in Atlanta. Although Du Bois identified the role of racial discrimination, economics, and social class in the growth of the city, his scholarship has been given relatively little attention. Sociological interests in race, class, and the city have been more importantly influenced by the Chicago School of sociology that was centered around the master sociologists, Robert Park and Ernest

Burgess. At the level of the city, these sociologists introduced a human eco-logical perspective that analogized the growth of the city to the competitive struggle of economic activities and human groups for survival within the phys-ical environment. The sifting and sorting processes, leading to the differenti-ation of economic activities and community areas which spatially took on the form of concentric zones, were explained by ecological processes of invasion, succession, and segregation. At the level of race relations, the ongoing contact and competition among racial and ethnic groups contained the expectations of conflict, accommodation, and assimilation. For these Chicago School sociol-ogists, the prejudices that instinctively and traditionally were reflected in social distance were to be challenged by subordinate group racial conflicts and antagonisms which indicated that the traditional social order was weakening, accommodation was no longer functional, and social distance was no longer effectively maintained. While many of these ideas of race, class, and the city influenced by the early Chicago School have been critiqued, the fundamental assumptions, concepts, and hypotheses continue to importantly influence how the contemporary experiences of race relations are interpreted. These classic perspectives have contributed important ideas of the "liberal expectancy" that have become parts of the dominant sociological belief system.

Scholars who study the city in its own right have usually grappled with a number of questions that are influenced by theory, research, public policy, and cultural beliefs. A partial list of these "burning questions" would include the following: How can the social structure of the city, suburb, and metrop-olis be best captured, described, and painted in terms of dimensionality? What are the changing macrosociological factors relevant to explaining the growth, decline, and revitalization of urban areas? What are the organiza-tional and disorganizational consequences of industrialization and urbaniza-tion for the quality of life of urban residents? To what extent are cities and their occupational opportunity structures sources of social mobility? How may differences in the residential movement and segregation of populations within and across urban areas be described and explained? To what extent do macrosociological factors of governmental organization, intergovernmental relationships, and public policy bear on ameliorating urban inequalities. The factors of race and class can intersect complexly with any of these concerns.

My interests in the sociologist, William Julius Wilson grew partly from my sociological interests and continuing interests in Black intellectuals. The convergence between my interests and those of Professor William Julius Wilson, from my perspective, is not accidental. I am a mature sociologist whose scholarly interests include urban sociology, race and ethnic relations, population, and theory; my research is focused on understanding how post-World War II and contemporary macrosociological changes such as corporate-administrative growth and deindustrialization, federal government expansion, and the construction of new communities in cities and suburbs of metropolitan areas were accompanied by changes in the socioeconomic and residential status of Blacks. Professor Wilson's insights have in no small part influenced my interests and understandings. While there is considerable convergence in Professor William Julius Wilson's interpretations of the Black experience in cities and my own interpretations, there are sufficient differences. This divergence appears to grow out of not only different theoretical and research orientations and interpretations, but also fundamentally different assessments of the post-World War II and contemporary experiences of Blacks in cities and the meanings of the intersection of race and class. I am not related to William Julius Wilson.

This study also grows out of my continuing interests in Black intellectuals in general and post-World War II Black sociologists specifically. It is an attempt to make sense of the status of sociology at the beginning of the twenty-first century and the persistent questions of class and race that continue to challenge democracy and social justice. In *The Crisis of the Negro Intellectual* (1967), Harold Cruse described the dualism in the challenges confronting Black intellectuals. On the one hand, these Black intellectuals were challenged to be acutely attuned to the American power structure, its cultural institutions, and structural changes in economics, politics, and social class in order to control or influence these. On the other hand, Black intellectuals were challenged to define and negotiate a role that would combine cultural and political criticism and include both programs and demands (Cruse 1967). Some of the directing questions which have structured this study include, but are not limited, to the following: How do Black sociologists address the continuing significance of race in American society and the complex challenges of assimilation, pluralism, nationalism, and separatism? What are the dilemmas for Black sociologists in the academy, as academic intellectuals, and in the larger society as public intellectuals? To what extent are these intellectual dilemmas reflected, reproduced, and resolved in sociological controversies and public issues? To what extent are these same intellectual dilemmas reflected, reproduced, and resolved in personal troubles and alienation? What are the continuing conflicts and how are these resolved?

As a graduate student, the critical and humanistic perspectives in the sociology of knowledge and sociology of sociology, as partly reflected in C. Wright Mills' *The Sociological Imagination* (1959), and *Power, Politics, and People,* (Horowitz 1963), Alvin Gouldner's *The Coming Crisis of Western Sociology* (1970), Peter Berger and Thomas Luckmann's *The Social Construction of Reality* (1970), and Thomas Kuhn's *The Structure of Scientific Revolutions* (1970), raised important questions and suggested some resolutions concerning the complex structural, cultural, and biographical relationships in the underside of sociology. The insights and controversies generated by the humanistic and critical perspectives in Harold Cruse's *The Crisis of the Negro Intellectual* (1967) and *Rebellion or Revolution* (1969), James Blackwell and Morris Janowitz's *The Black Sociologists* (1974), Joyce Ladner's *The Death of White Sociology* (1973), and the ongoing debates in *The Black Scholar* and *Black World* magazines were other important sources of sociological imagination and reflection which complemented my broader training in sociological theory and research methods.

At the same time, the presence of important social movements such as the civil rights movement and Black power movement, the antiwar movement, and the antiapartheid and "free South Africa" movements, awakened in me an appreciation of the role of consciousness, struggle, and human agency in history and the importance of understanding the ongoing syntheses of conflict and order in the reorganization of social reality. Among the sociologists, I became particularly inspired and energized by the promise of sociology contained in C. Wright Mill's *Sociological Imagination* and his numerous other works. It is from Mills' critique and appraisal of sociology that part of the renewal of sociology will take form. From numerous griots and teachers, I was also challenged to learn from the ancestors in order to provide a foundation for my better understanding of the present and charting directions for the future.

This examination is larger than a study of William Julius Wilson. It is in part an attempt to make sense of the status of sociology at the beginning of the twenty-first century and the persistent questions of class and race that continue to challenge democracy and social justice. A partial list of these "burning questions" include the following: How do sociologists address the complex challenges of postindustrial or corporate capitalism, liberalism, and conservatism at the beginning of the twenty-first century? What are the relevant social structures of politics, interest groups, association, and community that mediate between the society and the individual and how are they acted upon? To the extent that racism remains a complex, changing, and persistent structure of what many believe to be a deracialized American society, how do sociologists clarify and make sense of these contradictions? How does the persistence of racism bear on democracy and social justice and competing theories and ideologies of assimilation, pluralism, nationalism, and separatism? What are the unique challenges and dilemmas for the academic Black sociologist who is expert on racial matters, as an academic intellectual, or in the larger society, as a public intellectual? To what extent are these dilemmas reflected and reproduced in controversies and intellectual productions? What are the continuing conflicts and how are these resolved?

In approaching this study, I have pursued several aims. The first is to show that running through William Julius Wilson's scholarship is a complex treatment of changing post-civil rights race relations that is best theoretically understood as a discourse or dialogical approach. Through the use of socio-logical controversies, he has attempted to initiate a community of discourse among competing sociological and public policy perspectives that are often fragmented, isolated, and polarized. In his sociological analyses of race rela-tions, Wilson has initiated a discourse between the integration (social-order) and power conflict schools such as assimilation, pluralism, social class, and racial caste perspectives. In his analyses of social class, he has appropriated Marxian and neo-Marxian themes of social class and class formation and incorporated Weberian concepts and analyses of stratification. In his analyses of public policy, he has critically appraised and found common ground among liberal, neoliberal, neoconservative, and conservative perspectives of poverty, welfare, employment, and macroeconomics. This attempt at finding common ground, or the holistic perspective, runs through Wilson's early and later scholarship. This is a dynamic exercise of centrist analysis from what might be called, "the vital center."

A second aim is to show that Wilson's perspectives of race, class, and the city are importantly influenced by his formal perspectives and dialogical approach. Driving this is a pragmatic sociology focused on clarifying the meanings of human action, which is grounded on systematic theoretical explication and empirical research, and ultimately concerned with identifying systems of norms and values in human action. Understanding the formal and pragmatic sociology behind his analyses of race, class, and the city helps con-textualize and explain how Wilson has arrived at his generalizations. These perspectives appear to grow out of his training in the philosophy of the social sciences and his societal approach of race relations.

A third aim of this book examines the urban sociological questions that are resurrected and refocused in Wilson's analyses of Blacks in cities. In developing numerous descriptions, sketches, models, and theories of historic and contemporary race relations, Wilson has appropriated concepts and hypotheses from the Chicago School, critiques of the Chicago School, and at the same time gone beyond these to integrate competing perspectives. In his treatments of industrialization and class formation, Black migration, popula-tion growth and mobility, racial segregation and ghettoization, and the moral order of the Black community, he is "walking on old ground." His analyses of the role of industrialization in the class differentiation and integration of Blacks in the urban opportunity structure converge with and are informed by E. Franklin Frazier. In making sense of inner-city ghettos, Wilson draws from the classic concepts of Robert Park, Ernest Burgess, and Louis Wirth and reframes these as "concentration effects" and "social isolation." The pos-sibilities of Wilson's sociological treatments of Blacks in cities are primarily normative and center on his situating of changing race relations in its macrosociological contexts. The limitations of this analysis rest primarily on how he treats human and cultural agency, his understating of the continued role that structural features of racism, discrimination, and segregation have and the interrelations these have with social class.

There are several recurring themes relevant to the urban experience of African Americans that are addressed in Wilson's work that will be of concern here: (1) industrialization, urbanization, and the changing class structure of Blacks, (2) migration, population growth, and the social mobility of Blacks, (3) racial segregation and ghettoization, and (4) social isolation, concentration effects, and disorganization in the moral order of the inner city. Since beginning and revising this book, Wilson's *When Work Disappears* was published. It is examined in the context of his previous scholarship.

The fourth aim of this book is to provide a sociology of knowledge analysis which contextualizes the changing intellectual interests in William Julius Wilson's scholarship on race, class, and the city. The sociology of knowledge perspective begins from the premise that the intellectual products of scholars existentially grow out of historic and social contexts. For example, historically specific changing institutional contradictions such as the transformation of the U.S. economy from an industrially based to an increasingly postindustrial service based system, the reorganization of the government into an increasingly deregulated "new federalist" system, social class contradictions such as the declining influence of organized labor and industrial labor unions in American politics, and recent income trends which show increased inequality among higher and lower social classes are relevant to understanding sociological controversies. These changing institutional and class contradictions in turn have a bearing on how racial matters such as civil rights, affirmative action, immigration, the *Bell Curve* controversy, and the multiracial and multicultural debates are treated and discussed. The varied and complex ways in which scholars view their intellectual and professional objectives as connected or disconnected from these changing institutional and intergroup contradictions are importantly affected by their social integration and social consciousness.

From the microsociological perspective, the sociology of knowledge advances that intellectual products are social processes that enter a scholar's conversation and reflection including the internalized audience(s) and the collective ideas that in turn may be accepted, rejected, discarded, and reformulated. In examining sociological controversies, the dynamic of scholarly discourse may be examined in how knowledge is socially constructed and reconstructed based on logical rules, evidence, and critiques. The concepts, hypotheses, perspectives, arguments, theories, and rhetorical styles used by the scholar provide clues of the visible and invisible audiences and sociological rules.

Another premise in the sociology of knowledge advances that theories of social structure and social behavior can be understood sociologically as typical symbolic explanations associated with historically situated actions.

The sociologist, C. Wright Mills called these "situated actions" and "vocabularies of motive" and emphasized that the explanations current in sociology reflect the social experiences and social motives of American sociologists. Mills noted that earlier in the twentieth century, the typical vocabulary of explanation in mainstream sociology was singular and the motives expressed a small town or rural bias (Mills 1963). During the early post-World War II years, the sociological vocabulary was identified as a symbolic expression of a bureaucratic and administrative experience in life and work (Mills 1959). Currently, the vocabulary of explanation in mainstream sociology challenges scholars to creatively integrate and negotiate the varied assumptions of social control, which derive from a rational-legal bureaucratic *ethos* of modern industrialization, and the public policy values and norms of corporate liberalism and pragmatic conservatism.

It will be argued that William Julius Wilson's role as a leading public intellectual is partly understood by the changing situational factors that accompany his increased structural and cultural integration in academia and his role in sociological controversies. His social consciousness and analyses of race, class, and the city are complex and evolving. There are subtle changes in emphasis in the paradigms used by him that in turn influence his perceptions, the questions asked, and the concepts and language used for formalizing his accounts. Accompanying changes in his professional career, his theorizing moves from a complex dialectic using functionalist, symbolic interaction, power-conflict and social history perspectives to a relatively more conservative social control model incorporating the earlier perspectives with stronger political economy, urban ecological, and social capital perspectives. Over time, his public presentation or persona will also undergo symbolic changes.

At the same time, there are strong elements of persistence in his scholarship. Throughout his scholarship, there is a continuing concern to address the complex relationships between changing macrosociological structures of the economy, government, and urban community and changes in racial and ethnic relations. The societal or macrosociological argument running throughout his work remains fundamentally intact. While he maintains interests in race relations, he wants to go beyond race relations to address larger societal concerns. Driving this is a pragmatic sociology focused on the meanings of human action, grounded on systematic theoretical explication and empirical research, which is ultimately concerned with identifying and clarifying systems of norms and values in human action. Sociological controversies and discourses bearing on race, class, and public policy are the arenas for this pragmatic sociology.

The fifth aim of this book focuses on Wilson's vision of American society and the roles that sociologists and sociology might play in social reform.

The promise of sociology draws primarily on its role in formulating public issues and policy research. Driving this is a recognition that the future of sociology will increasingly be based on the extent which sociological theories, hypotheses, and concepts are used in the formulation and discussion of public-policy issues and the extent which sociological research broadens its domain of policy relevant scholarship and becomes more pragmatic, flexible, and accessible. Although the role of sociology in public policy has long been recognized as an important goal, how this becomes articulated in both theory and practice has diverse and competing directions. The age-old questions of "knowledge for what" and "knowledge for whom" continue to be unresolved. Wilson provides one strategy of clarification for these questions. Through sociological controversy, Wilson introduces a refocused liberal discourse that brings together social science and public policy perspectives.

ACKNOWLEDGMENTS

This manuscript has truly been a social construction. Over the course of this investigation, I have incurred more debts than I have acknowledged here. Earlier drafts of this manuscript benefited from the reviews by Margaret Anderson, Eduardo Bonilla-Silva, James Conyers, John Farley, Carl Jorgensen, Anthony Orum, Gordon Morgan, John Stanfield, Stephen Steinberg, and Charles Tilly. Their very constructive, helpful, and detailed suggestions and criticisms have helped the revisions in immeasurable ways.

At the University of Wisconsin-Milwaukee, where I have taught for the past fifteen years in the department of sociology and urban studies program, Lakshmi Bharadwaj, Ron Edari, Don Green, Ann Greer, Eleanor Miller, Joan Moore, Don Noel, Stacey Oliker, Eric Rambo, Harold Rose, Gregory Squires, William Velez, and John Zipp have been delightful colleagues. They have taken time from their busy schedules to either read drafts or listen to the arguments in brown bags. Over the years, graduate students in the urban social structure seminar at the University of Wisconsin-Milwaukee discussed many of the issues contained in the book and freshened my interests and curiosity.

Also the anonymous reviewers at the State University of New York Press provided several constructive criticisms and recommendations that have tremendously improved this manuscript. These recommendations helped me to rethink and refocus parts of the study. The encouragement from these same anonymous reviewers energized my productivity.

William Julius Wilson is to be generously thanked for providing an interview. He has taken time from a very busy schedule to address several questions and has also provided unpublished papers and materials that have been useful in these efforts. He also provided comments and corrections for an earlier draft of the manuscript. The thoroughness, carefulness, and genuine interest shared by him in this project have helped energize its completion. Through secondary sources, Wilson has provided a trail of public interviews that stretch over twenty years. The sociological perspectives and discussions of race and class introduced by him have in part influenced my sociological imagination.

Other scholars interviewed in connection with this include Lewis Killian, Charles Willie, Douglas Massey, Edgar Epps, Alphonso Pinkney, Robert Solow, Sue Model, Lew Walker, Doris Wilkinson, and Timuel Black. Papers based on this research have been presented to professional conferences at the American Sociological Association, the Society for the Study of Social Problems, the Association of Social and Behavioral Scientists, and the Midwest Sociological Society. To the numerous other persons that I have talked to concerning this scholarship that are not mentioned, thank you.

I am particularly indebted to the University of Wisconsin-Milwaukee for providing a paid sabbatical during the academic year 1998–1999 which allowed me to complete major portions of the book. Without the sabbatical, it is doubtful whether this project would be completed.

My family has been a continuing source of nurturing, support, and love through the years. For my parents, Frank Harold Wilson, Sr., and Ruth Johnson Wilson, my brother, Charles Edgar Wilson, and all of my extended family, thank you. The greatest appreciation is expressed to my wife, Edie Adekunle-Wilson, who has been an anchor of love, understanding, and reassurance during this intellectual journey. Her encouragement, inspiration, devotion, and patience have added to the enjoyment of this project. She has been the most important person in this effort.

I have approached this project with both sympathy and criticism. The search for truth and meaning has been paramount. Any strengths that this book may have are due to the generous and constructive contributions of the numerous scholars who have taken time from their busy schedules for interviews, to read earlier drafts of the manuscript, discuss the issues, and help in various ways. Of course, I alone am responsible for any shortcomings in this book.

CHAPTER 1

THE SHADOW BEHIND THE ACT

THE BEGINNINGS OF A BLACK SCHOLAR

William Julius Wilson's journey as a sociologist begins during the years of the Great Depression, the New Deal recovery, and World War II. His early nurturing and growing up take place in the Middle Ground of western Pennsylvania—an area that is nested geographically and socially between the northeastern and midwestern United States. Wilson was born on December 20, 1935 in Derry township, Pennsylvania. He is the oldest of six children born to Esco Wilson and Pauline Bracey Wilson; he grew up in a community named Bairdstown (H. West 1979; Abramowitz 1991). According to Wilson, "when we were growing up, we considered Bairdstown a suburb of Blairsville. . . . The two communities were separated by a river." (W. J. Wilson, letter to author, July 31, 2000). Today, Bairdstown no longer exists. Its identity is connected with Blairsville and Derry township.

Derry township is a small, rural nonfarm community in Westmoreland County roughly fifty miles east of Pittsburgh. The social structure of this working-class community in a mining district of western Pennsylvania was largely made up of workers in operatives, crafts, and laboring lines of work. Before the United States entry into World War II, Derry township's recovery in 1940 from the Great Depression was reflected in nearly 87 percent of its male labor force employed and 13 percent of its male labor force unemployed. The median years of school completed by adult residents (twenty-five years and older) in 1940 was 7.4 years and females made up roughly 20 percent of the work force. Derry township contained a diverse ethnic community of families largely made up of persons of English American, German American, Irish American, and Italian American ancestry.

During Wilson's growing-up years, Derry township contained a proportionately small Black population. According to 1940 census figures, 280 Blacks were represented among the town's more than fourteen thousand residents. Wilson notes: "Blacks were spread throughout Derry township and no distinctive Black community existed" (W. J. Wilson, interview by author, June

1

16, 1997). Although Blacks were dispersed and integrated in Derry township, there also appears to have been social networks among Blacks and a Black church. Despite the integration, Wilson was not insulated from racial prejudice and discrimination. In one interview, he shares that "I was called 'nigger' by the older boys, and I got into some fights triggered by racial slurs" (Remnick 1996, 99). While experiencing some discrimination in the stores, he states: "he did not experience segregation nor feel especially deprived" (Remnick 1996, 99).

Economic and social circumstances more than race appear to have influenced his perceptions, consciousness, and outlook on life. His father worked regularly and hard as a laborer in the coal mines and steel mills within the Pittsburgh area. When Wilson was thirteen, his father died at age thirty-nine of lung disease. Following his father's death, his family had financial difficulties. Briefly the Wilson family collected relief; to supplement her family's needs, his mother worked part-time cleaning houses (Remnick 1996; Abramowitz 1991). In one interview he indicated: "We used to go hungry a lot. It was real poverty. We were struggling all the time" (Remnick 1996, 99). Elsewhere he explained: "The vegetables from our garden literally kept us from starving" (Reynolds 1992, 84), and "For a family of seven, we had one quart of milk a week" (Remnick, 1996). Despite growing up poor, Wilson emphasized that in Derry township he did not feel deprived or trapped in poverty. Nor did he experience the "crowded conditions, crime, drugs, and the sense of being imprisoned" (Moyers 1989, 80).

A close, nurturing, and mutually supportive extended family figured importantly in Wilson's expectations, achievements, and aspirations. His parents worked regularly and hard and the children in the Wilson family grew up with their lives organized around work. While neither of his parents completed high school and were materially poor, both nurtured the expectation that William and his brothers and sisters would go on to college. He described his family as an extremely close one; his mother encouraged her children by creating a study time. While she knitted, they would all sit around the table and do their homework (Abramowitz 1991, B2). While we were growing up he notes, "All we ever heard from our mother was talk of going to college" (Hollie West 1979, 70). Reinforcing this, the teachers in his schools were described as encouraging and "never gave up on us" (Remnick 1996, 99).

Although he was expected to do well in school and go on to college, there were sometimes competing pressures. As a youngster, he was at times more interested in making the football team than getting good grades (Abramowitz 1991, B1). One may infer that as the oldest male child, he had important expectations and responsibilities with respect to school, family, and work. He was expected to be a role model for his younger siblings. One may also safely infer that William was a serious and prepared student whose educational promise and preparation were high but only partly actualized. The actualization of these expectations and personal ambitions in achievement, scholarship, and academic recognition would occur over three decades.

Within his extended family, his aunt, Janice Wardlaw played an important role in supporting his college education. According to Wilson, his father had helped pay his Aunt Janice Wardlaw's tuition; she was the first person to complete college within the extended family and she lived in New York. In return, Aunt Janice agreed to help finance William's college tuition. His aunt, who is now deceased, was a former social worker and a psychiatric social worker; she held two master's degrees. She served as an important role model, for she took William to museums and libraries during his summer visits in New York. Janice Wardlaw's husband introduced him to boy scouting. When he completed high school, his aunt invited him to live in New York City with her family. She introduced him to her office colleagues and others in the city (Hollie West 1979, 74). Aunt Janice inspired and intellectually challenged him by giving him books and by "talking constantly about the importance of ambition and creativity" (Moyers 1989; Remnick 1996). Through Wilson's encouragement and support, each of his younger brothers and sisters earned at least a bachelor's degree. His siblings include: a brother who is a college administrator, a brother who is a mathematician and computer consultant for an airline, a sister with the Ph.D. who teaches college, and two sisters with nursing degrees. One of the latter sisters also has a master's degree in business administration. The possibilities of achievement and mobility through education appear to grow out of his family's expectations and personal life experiences; they will constitute an important norm in his analyses of race relations and prescriptions of social policy.

Wilson attended Wilberforce University with a scholarship from his church and additional financial support from his aunt. Wilberforce University has the distinction of being the oldest historically Black institution of higher education and one of the schools where W. E. B. Du Bois, the eminent sociologist and historian, taught earlier in the twentieth century. At Wilberforce, he initially considered majoring in business administration, however, he changed his major after taking his first sociology courses. Among his teachers at Wilberforce, Professor Maxwell Brooks is mentioned as capturing his sociological interests with courses in social problems and race (Remnick 1996).

Maxwell Brooks was a consummate scholar and one of the first Blacks to receive a Ph.D. in sociology from Ohio State University. At Wilberforce during the 1950s, Professor Brooks and the department of sociology were synonymous. Brooks was a generalist who taught courses such as theory, history of social thought, research methods, race relations, social movements, and social disorganization. Brooks was formal, well-dressed, dispassionate, and careful in both his manner and teaching. His lectures were well-formulated. In this church-based university, Brooks was fiercely independent, scientific, and heretical in orientation (L. Walker, interview by the author, April 13, 1998). Wilson remembers him as having an interest in McCarthyism (Remnick 1996).

It is significant that Maxwell Brooks was both a mentor and role model for Wilson. As the top student in his class, Brooks offered him a teaching assistantship (W. J. Wilson, interview by the author, June 16, 1997). Brooks also sponsored Wilson as a member into the honor society, "Sword and Shield" (L. Walker, interview by the author, April 13, 1998). Working under Brooks, he developed the holistic perspective that would influence his sociological imagination and analyses of social problems (W. J. Wilson, interview by the author, June 16, 1997). Whether consciously or unconsciously, Wilson appears to have partly modeled his broad intellectual interests and professional image after Maxwell Brooks.

Outside the classroom, Wilson was a campus leader involved in student government and politics. He pledged and became a member of the Omega Psi Phi fraternity. Although Wilberforce was a small campus at this time (roughly three hundred students), the campus environment was highly competitive, socially close, and encouraged participation in extracurricular and service activities. The academic and social environment appears to have been nurturing and supportive for him. It is during the Wilberforce years that he met and dated Mildred Hood who he married in 1957. From this marriage he has two daughters, Colleen and Lisa.

After graduating from Wilberforce, Wilson served two years in the United States Army between 1958 and 1960 earning the rank of specialist fourth class. In the United States Army, he earned the Meritorious Service Award. It is significant that while stationed at Fort Bliss, Texas he took an officer's training course in social psychology where he excelled as the top student. While he was in the army, his wife, Mildred Hood Wilson was living and working in Toledo, Ohio (W. J. Wilson, interview by the author, June 16, 1997).

Following his discharge from the army, William's sociological training and career advanced very rapidly. His transition from the army to graduate school was partly enabled by Professor Maxwell Brooks who knew a Professor Longsworth at Bowling Green University, who in turn offered him a fellowship. Bowling Green University's closeness to Toledo was important for it enabled Wilson to enjoy his family and pursue scholarly matters. He studied for and received a master's degree in sociology at Bowling Green State University in Ohio in 1961. His master's thesis was entitled, "A Study of Attitudes of the Protestant Pastors of Church and Sect Type Religious Organizations in the City of Toledo Toward Militarism and Pacifism." This focused on liberal and fundamentalist religiosity and the relationship between political attitudes and human action. Among the intellectual influences at Bowling Green on his scholarship were Arthur Neal, Joseph Perry, and Frank Miles. The holistic approach in the thesis also shows the earlier influences of Maxwell Brooks.

THE WASHINGTON STATE YEARS

From Bowling Green, Wilson went directly to Washington State University in Pullman, Washington to the Ph.D. program. Washington State during the 1960s and early 1970s was one of the leading research and training centers in sociology to actively recruit Black graduate students. During these years, Washington State University graduated more Black doctorates in sociology than any university in the country. Professor T. H. Kennedy, an important faculty member, was influencial in recruiting Blacks for the doctoral program.

At Washington State, Wilson initially wanted to study social stratification, however, the late Richard Ogles, a former professor of sociology at Washington State and an important intellectual influence, helped to refocus his interest. According to Wilson, Richard Ogles was "one of the most brilliant theoretical methodologists in the social sciences." Ogles introduced Wilson to the writings of the philosophers of science Ernest Nagel, Karl Hempel, and Gustav Bergman (W. J. Wilson, interview by the author, June 16, 1997). As a doctoral student, his studies principally concentrated on theory construction, the logic of sociological inquiry, and the philosophy of social sciences (Wilson 1986, 4–5). Theoretically, Wilson was impressed with the precision in the thinking in the philosophy of science, for sociologists were seen as less precise in their thinking. During these years, he studied the philosophies of science and scientific theories of evaluation. In these studies, he explains that "we would apply the context of validation of concepts and explanations and the context of data and exploration" (W. J. Wilson, interview by the author, June 16, 1997).

His dissertation and early publications indicate a continuing interest with formal theoretical concerns (Wilson and Dumont 1968; Dumont and Wilson 1967; Wilson, Sofios, and Ogles 1964). Wilson received the Bobbs-Merrill award as the outstanding graduate student in the department of sociology (1963) and his Ph.D. in 1965 from Washington State University. Reflecting on the Washington State years, he notes: "I became a star out there and came into my own" (Remnick 1996, 99).

In his earliest sociological publications, Wilson addresses the scientific status of sociological theory with respect to the structures of explanation, significance of concepts, and the nature of evidence (Wilson and Dumont 1968; Dumont and Wilson 1967). In these writings, he takes issue with sociological approaches based on abstract empiricism, the new causal sociology, and logical positivism. He asks whether the evaluative criteria that are used in formal examinations of the social science logic of inquiry are methodologically distinct from the natural and physical sciences and what bearing these have on the proper construction of social theory. While arguing that the use of more rigorous evaluative criteria in theory construction functions to make explicit the logical and empirical status of theorists and help evaluate their claims, Wilson sees two paths in theory that may be based largely on rigorous evaluative criteria, for example, (1) sociology may eliminate from inquiry all that does not conform with these standards; and (2) sociology may develop a practical program for selecting and developing those aspects of sociological theory that show promise of eventual conformity with these criteria. Wilson sees the first path as problematic, excessive, and to be resisted because it will result in both "good" and "bad" sociology being thrown out. The correct path is more pragmatic. In this practical program of sociology, Wilson suggests bases or standards for the selection, evaluation, and utilization of concepts in sociological theories (Dumont and Wilson 1967).

For Wilson, the forms of sociological theories run the continuum between implicit and explicit construction. What distinguishes these explicit theories from implicit theories is the presence of epistemic and constitutive significance where "concepts are connected either directly or indirectly, with observables by rules of correspondence that have been empirically justified" (Dumont and Wilson 1967, 987). Implicit theories are characterized by "isolated abstract concepts that have an ambiguity and openness of meanings while affording no clear specification as to how or why they were derived." These implicit theories do not have a definitive rationale for the use of indicators. In between implicit and explicit theories is the theory sketch—"a more or less vague indication of the laws and initial conditions considered as relevant to be later filled out into a full explanation." He notes, "the connection between the observable concepts and theoretical concepts is only presumed to represent an empirical relation." Explicit theories contain concepts with epistemic and constitutive significance alongside rationales for the use of correspondence rules. Explication consists of both meaning analysis and empirical analysis. Meaning analysis involves surveying the literature to "cull out the most basic assumptions inherent in various meanings of concepts." Empirical analysis refers to submitting meaning analysis to direct empirical test (Dumont and Wilson 1967, 988–990).

Wilson's sociology is an analysis of the meanings of human action that should be grounded upon systematic theoretical explication and empirical research. This sociology of human action is primarily based on an idealistic and humanistic orientation that is ultimately concerned with identifying and clarifying normative systems and values. There is a pragmatism built in of

standards for the selection, evaluation, and utilization of concepts in sociological theories.

Elements of this formal theory, human action, scientific theory of evaluation and pragmatism will remain in later writings. Although he was initially
interested in stratification, there are no writings during these years focused
on social class or race relations.

THE AMHERST YEARS

Wilson's first academic appointment was as an Assistant Professor at the University of Massachusetts, Amherst in 1965. The University of Massachusetts,
Amherst is the leading public university in New England and the department
of sociology is nationally recognized. The academic community in the sociology department was liberal and was characterized by close working relationships with faculty at other nearby institutions such as Smith College,
Mount Holyoke, and Williams College. Collegially, it was a competitive and
supportive environment.

For Wilson, it is significant that his initial academic and tenure
appointment at the University of Massachusetts preceded the initiation of
affirmative action in higher education. In one interview he states that when
he was hired, "no one questioned whether it was because I was Black"
(Reynolds 1992, 84). Elsewhere he adds: "The Sociology Department was
pleasantly surprised to find out he was Black. Based on reading his resume,
there was nothing to indicate in terms of research specialties and interests
that he was Black" (W. J. Wilson, interview by the author, June 16, 1997). As
a scholar, Wilson did very well at the University of Massachusetts and
received tenure and promotion to associate professor without the slightest
difficulty. During the Amherst years, Wilson was recognized as a master
teacher and in 1970 won the Distinguished Teaching Award (S. Model, letter
to author, April 16, 1990).

Although earlier theoretical interests in the philosophy of social science
and formal theory would remain, Wilson's sociological concerns would additionally be influenced by events outside the academy. According to Wilson:

> In my last two years as a graduate student in the mid-1960s I, like most
> Blacks, was caught up in the spirit of the Civil Rights Revolution and was
> encouraged by the changes in social structure that led to increasing oppor-
> tunities for Black Americans. I also followed with intense interest the ghetto
> riots in Watts, Newark, and Detroit. And although at this point I had not
> developed a serious academic interest in the field of race and ethnic rela-
> tions, my intellectual curiosity for the subject, fed by the escalating racial
> protest and my sense of the changing social structure for Blacks in America,
> was rising so rapidly that by the time I accepted my full-time academic job

as an Assistant-Professor of Sociology at the University of Massachusetts, Amherst in the fall of 1965, I had firmly decided to develop a field of specialization in that area. (Wilson 1988, 81)

The burning concerns driving Wilson's interests in racial and ethnic relations would be the relative lack of theory, social history, and cross-cultural studies in the area. However, he was not interested in being a sociologist who was known for his work in race relations, but in fact had broader concerns of connecting a more holistic societal analysis with racial and ethnic stratification.

In addition to teaching courses in race and ethnic relations, Wilson taught a course in the philosophy of social science. During these years, Wilson was a scholar who was intellectually and socially integrated into the worlds of the sociology department, the Black Studies movement, and larger academic concerns of an interdisciplinary nature. The focus and targeted audiences of his publications show that he was connected with the worlds of both White and Black scholars. Colleagues within the University of Massachusetts, sociology department who Wilson regularly interacted with included: Lewis Killian, Milton Gordon, and Charles Page. A critical mass of Black scholars on campus included: Michael Thelwell, William Darrity, Johnetta Cole, and Castellano Turner.

Wilson was at Amherst during a period of Black student unrest and protest. Here he played a significant role as a negotiator between sides and was an effective mediator. He was involved in the establishment of the Committee for the Collegiate Education of Black Students (currently titled Committee for the Collegiate Education of Black and Minority Students). This organization was involved in recruiting and support programs such as academic counseling, tutoring, and monitoring (S. Model, letter to the author, April 16, 1990).

Drawing from these experiences at the University of Massachusetts and the controversies of Black studies and Black recruitment in northern universities, he addresses the crisis facing Black students, faculty, and training institutes of Black studies in historically Black colleges and White universities during the late 1960s (Wilson 1970). In an article entitled, "New Creation or Familiar Death," Wilson forcefully responds to Vincent Harding's challenge for Black students and faculty in the North to create meaningful Black experiences on predominantly White campuses. He envisions numerous strategies of Blacks becoming incorporated in these programs "to recruit, enroll, and financially aid so-called high risk and forgotten Black students from urban ghettos, the development of Afro-American studies programs, and the development of creative institutional partnerships and consortium between northern White universities and Black universities with respect to faculty and community development." While recognizing that White universities have vested interests in "institutional protection," he emphasizes that Black faculty and students in the North continue to pressure their universities to recruit nontraditional Black students having intellectual potential that would be evaluated as academically marginal based on conventional White middle-class standards (Wilson 1970, 9). While recognizing the possibilities that some Black universities and colleges might play in developing Black studies curriculum and training faculty in these disciplines such as The Institute of the Black World in Atlanta, Wilson envisions a larger and more important role that northern universities and Black faculty on these campuses might play within these activities in the future.

Another publication written during the Amherst years exemplifies the complex and macrosociological perspectives that would become refocused and polished during the Chicago years. In an essay entitled, "Race Relations Models and Ghetto Experience," he not only reviewed the economic class, assimilation, and colonial models, but also assessed their adequacy in accounting for the 1960s collective responses by Black ghetto residents to racial subjugation (Wilson 1972). Additionally, he addressed the relevance of these models in accounting for the content and character of cultural and revolutionary nationalism and Black liberation movements. It is instructive to note that this essay was primarily based around Harold Cruse's discussion of the failure of American sociologists to comprehend the basis of racial conflict (Cruse 1969). Wilson draws inspiration from this and both dialectically and eclectically weaves together a discussion of the possibilities and limitations of the different models. He concludes that no one model can be considered as adequate and possibly new models will be needed to account for the relationships among changing social structure, social movements, and racial relations:

> It could be that the future course of events will bring an indefinite period of polarization between races; yet in view of the fact that as sociologists we were sadly ill-prepared to anticipate or explain the racial explosions of the late 1960s, we should make every effort to free ourselves of positions that tend to be too restrictive in the explanation of racial behavior. In some cases, therefore, it may be necessary to investigate a particular problem with a multi-model approach, in another situation a single model may suffice. Finally, in some instances none of the existing models may apply and hence altogether new propositions have to be constructed to arrive at a satisfactory explanation. In fine, a recognition of the limitations of the existing models of race behavior could be a crucial first step in improving our overall knowledge and in broadening our imagination. (Wilson 1972, 271)

Wilson was already proposing a theoretical agenda that would have arching concerns and bring together into dialogue several perspectives that are usually separated, if not polarized, in academic sociology. This sociological craftsmanship involved a complex and eclectic approach of theory construction that frequently incorporates retroductive logic. The discussion of these models of race relations would increasingly take place in the "vital center."

It should be noted that while at Amherst, Wilson was not involved in empirically researching issues of race. Based on his scholarship at the University of Massachusetts-Amherst, there is little to suggest that primary empirical research was more than a secondary concern in grounding his sociological imagination. As a theoretician, Wilson has usually summarized and synthesized the research of other sociologists and integrated these findings with his own observations. From these, he has explicated theories, theory sketches, hypotheses, and concepts. The primary empirical research informing his discussions would come after his publication of *The Truly Disadvantaged: The Inner City, the Underclass and Public Policy* (1987) and in *When Work Disappears: The World of the New Urban Poor* (1996).

It is significant that Wilson's critique of the existing state of theory in race relations would draw from some of the more independent and alternative models coming out of sociology during the late 1960s and early 1970s such as Lewis Killian, Stanley Lieberson, Richard Schermerhorn, Robert Blauner, Milton Gordon, Pierre van den Berghe, and Ira Katznelson. Also initially important in influencing Wilson's theoretical understandings would be the work of two African American scholars: Harold Cruse (author of *The Crisis of the Negro Intellectual* (1967), *Rebellion or Revolution* (1969), *and Plural but Equal: Blacks and Minorities in America's Plural Society* (1987)); Oliver Cromwell Cox (author of *Caste, Class, and Race: A Study of Social Dynamics* (1948), *Foundations of Capitalism, and Capitalism as a System*). These scholars provided critical political-economy analyses of capitalism focused on cultural and structural aspects of race relations. Although Wilson would acknowledge the importance of these African American scholars early in his career, they appear to have less direct influences in later work. Two other African-American scholars that he would draw from substantially in conceptualizations of the urban underclass would be the sociologist, E. Franklin Frazier and the social psychologist, Kenneth Clark.

Wilson began writing *Power, Racism, and Privilege: Race Relations in Theoretical and Sociohistorical Perspectives* at Amherst. The lecture notes and discussions from a comprehensive seminar on racial stratification entitled, "The Black Man in America" represented the foundations of this book. In the early 1980s, the University of Massachusetts-Amherst awarded William Wilson an honorary doctorate.

THE SOCIOLOGY DEPARTMENT AT THE
UNIVERSITY OF CHICAGO

The University of Chicago has been centrally involved in the history and development of sociology. The traditions in the department of sociology or the Chicago School are based on integrating sociological theory with systematic observation and empirical data and connecting sociological theory with public policy issues. Structurally, the department has been a interdisciplinary one drawing from the theoretical and research interests of faculty from other disciplines in the social sciences such as economics, political science, geography, anthropology, and psychology, and humanities disciplines such as literature, philosophy, and history, and professions such as education, social work, and planning.

From the turn of the century to the early 1930s, the Chicago school of sociology and its pioneers such as Albion Small, W. I. Thomas, Robert Park, Ernest Burgess, Louis Wirth, George Herbert Mead, and William Ogburn established a pragmatic and liberal tradition of social scientific investigation that linked the university with the urban community and the growing industrial society (Faris 1967). This pragmatic-liberal approach contrasted sharply with the more philosophical, historical, and social ethics approaches of sociology within older universities in the eastern United States. The dominance of Chicago sociology in the early history of the discipline would be exemplified by the quality and quantity of Ph.D.'s trained, the institutionalization of the American Sociological Society and the publication, *The American Journal of Sociology*, the large representation of University of Chicago faculty and graduates among the officers of the American Sociological Society (and later American Sociological Association), and the intellectual dominance of its theories, models, and concepts (Smith 1988; Faris 1967).

Early on, the Chicago School became a leading center for special programs such as urban sociology, human ecology, collective behavior, social change, demography, social psychology, and race relations. At this time, the Chicago School was the most democratic and accessible university in the graduate training of Black sociologists with Ph.D. degrees. Among its graduates, during the 1920s and 1930s, were some of the leading Black sociologists of the twentieth century including: Charles S. Johnson, E. Franklin Frazier, Horace Cayton, and Oliver Cromwell Cox (Bracey, Meier, Rudwick 1971, 7–11). The interdisciplinary community included other Black scholars such as Allison Davis and St. Clair Drake. The Chicago School was the first sociology program to integrate into its research training Black faculty and students from traditionally Black universities and colleges (Jones 1974; S. Smith 1974). The influence of the Chicago School is reflected in many important sociological studies on Black urban life and the ghetto.

The scientific sociology developed by the pioneers at the University of Chicago studied urbanization and race and ethnic relations using cross-national and universalistic frameworks. Sociologists such as Robert Park emphasized methodologies taken from the anthropological techniques of participant observation and the case study approach of investigation while valuing understandings of the historic background of social institutions. Park's theorizing included not only ecological concepts that were manifest in the city as a social and moral order, but also the dynamics of race and ethnic contacts as reflected in the race relations cycle. Park's theorizing included organismic assumptions of a biosocial urban community driven by ecological processes of invasion, succession, dominance, and segregation (Coser 1971, 363–364), and social processes of competition, conflict, accommodation, and assimilation (Coser 1971, 359). In Burgess' theorizing, the growth of the city and its spatial structuring into zones and natural areas were accompanied by ecological processes of invasion and succession (Burgess 1925).

Built into both Park's, Burgess' and other pioneers writings were attempts at holistic theory construction that importantly incorporated macrosociological-level conceptualizations of community organization and microsociological models of social psychological and interactive bases of urban life. There was an attempt to identify the interpsychic forms of inter-group life in the city and link these with population factors—size, density, heterogeneity, social organization—disorganization, reorganization, and larger societal forces—technology, and division of labor. Park developed a "race relations cycle" describing that when diverse races come into contact, competition, conflict, accommodation, and assimilation invariably take place. Although prejudice and antagonisms occurred in these early stages, tolerance, interracial cooperation, and acculturation were predicted to occur later. Built into Burgess and Park's theorizing and concepts was a formalism that contained analytically interrelated but separated social processes of competition, conflict, accommodation, and assimilation that were related to social structures of the economy, political order, social organization, personality and cultural heritage respectively (Martindale 1981, 238–241).

After the Great Depression of the 1930s, the University of Chicago continued to play a leading role in the growth of higher education, the social and behavioral sciences, and the professionalization and training of sociologists. However, since the "mini-revolution" of academic sociology in 1935, the dominance of the Chicago School has been increasingly challenged. First, after World War II, the federal government and private philanthropy played much larger roles in supporting social science research. According to Martin Bulmer, this postwar sociology, which was increasingly applied sociology, became more focused on the nation-state, the welfare state, market research, and public opinion than the earlier Chicago research programs which were more targeted on problems of urban social structure (Bulmer 1992, 335). Although the growth of these research resources greatly benefited the University of Chicago, these developments helped to decentralize the research and training centers of social science. Nationally, the status of social science theory and research became more bureaucratized, differentiated, specialized, and separated during these years. Second, new centers such as Harvard University, Columbia University, University of California, Berkeley, University of Michigan, University of Wisconsin, and University of North Carolina incorporated many of the newer theoretical and research approaches as well as appropriated traditional ones that earlier were centralized at the University of Chicago. The development of structural functional theory—the leading post-World War II sociological theory—was primarily based at Harvard and Columbia. Some centers, such as University of Michigan and University of Wisconsin, developed empirical research training programs, institutes, and research niches. Third, there are arguments that the failure of Chicago social scientists to predict the economic depression of the 1930s and the rise of political movements in Europe, led to a search for new directions of theory and policy rationales outside of the liberal and pragmatic parameters of the University of Chicago, which had implications for Chicago sociology. These new social theories, which were also liberal and pragmatic, emphasized to a greater degree the state intervention and social policy themes characterizing the New Deal and the Keynesian economic order than the older social theories which had more social Darwin and laissez-faire themes. Fourth, with the publication of Gunnar Myrdal's *An American Dilemma: The Negro Problem in Modern Democracy* (1944), the study of race relations received a new consensus and interpretation that replaced the earlier intergroup perspectives of the Chicago School. The study of African Americans and race relations, traditionally based in southern schools, the historically Black colleges, and the University of Chicago, would gain new legitimacy in leading northern universities during the post-World War II years. Following Robert Park's moving to Fisk University during his later years, the status of the race relations specialty at the Chicago School lost ground during the 1940s and 1950s.

During the post-World War II period, mainstream urban sociology continued to be influenced by the classical ecological perspectives while it was refocused. Structural-functionalist and complex organizational perspectives also significantly informed this human ecology. The rapid growth of metropolitan areas and the suburbs, rather than the growth of the city, constituted its new starting point. Unlike the pioneering University of Chicago sociologists who identified the city as a primary focus of research, these theorists were more broadly concerned with studying the nature, variation, and interrelations of territorially based or community forms (Hawley 1950; Duncan 1959; Hawley 1981). In this more systems-oriented human ecology, with its increasing emphases of scientific holism, functionalism, and systems analysis, research shifted to the functional relationships that communities and urban systems played in the larger division of labor and urban hierarchy. Similar to the classical Chicago sociology, the focus of macrosociological change in these conceptualizations retained traditional ecological concerns with population redistribution in their focus on the dynamics of growth/decline, concentration/deconcentration, centralization/decentralization and convergence/divergence that were shaped by Durkheimian assumptions of equilibrium and quantitative change. Post-World War II human ecology retained urban ecology's focus on the internal structure of urban communities by maintaining concerns with the residential distribution of populations by class, race, and status. The most frequently identified dimensions of Blacks in cities—residential segregation and social inequality—were intertwined with social policy questions such as civil rights, civil disorders, and the War on Poverty.

The University of Chicago's department of sociology reestablished much of its stature as a theoretical, research, and training center at the cutting edge of professional sociology during the late 1960s and 1970s. At a time when structural functional theory—the leading paradigm of post-World War II sociology—experienced a crisis of confidence, the University of Chicago institutionally consolidated new and traditional approaches in sociology via its faculty, research programs, and students. Alongside the traditional academic specialties in social psychology, urban sociology, demography and human ecology, social organization, and social change, the strong interdisciplinary relationships within the department and across the social sciences were increasingly reflected in specialties such as sociological practice/social policy, mathematical sociology, comparative sociology, economy and society, philosophy of the social sciences, and theory.

Reflecting the stronger relationships among the economy, state, and academy, the Chicago School became a leader in the increased use of social forecasting based on social indicators and the "new causal theory." Through the presence of sociologists such as Morris Janowitz, Peter Blau, James Coleman, Stanley Lieberson, Peter Rossi, William Julius Wilson, Donald Bogue, Gerald Suttles, and the economist Gary Becker, Chicago sociology reasserted itself as a leader in comparative and macrosociology, urban sociology, demography and human ecology, theory, quantitative sociology, and qualitative methodological approaches.

Among these scholars, Morris Janowitz became an important post-World War II theoretical leader in macrosociology bringing together the Chicago traditions of Robert Park, Louis Wirth, and William F. Ogburn, structural functionalism, other social science disciplines, and public policy (D. Smith 1988, 201). Through Morris Janowitz, attention was refocused on the modern metropolis and the contributions made to social control by macrosociological institutions such as industry, government, the military, education, and community institutions (D. Smith 1988, 201). At the same time, Janowitz encouraged a model for increasing the role of sociologists in social policy. According to Dennis Smith, this model focused on the collection and presentation of social trends, the testing of specific hypotheses about institutions and social problems, the development of generalizations and sensitizing concepts, the evaluation of actual and proposed strategies of social intervention, and the articulation of complex models of society to encourage empirical research on institutions and social problems (D. Smith 1988, 201–202).

By the 1980s, the Chicago School would also become one of the leaders in the study of poverty and inequality, rational choice social economics, gender and society, and social history. William Julius Wilson would play an important role in refocusing national attention on urban poverty through *The Truly Disadvantaged* and research on inner-city poverty through the Center for the Study of Urban Inequality, which he founded and directed. Wilson's macrosociology is importantly influenced by Janowitz's model of the role of social scientists in social policy.

WILLIAM JULIUS WILSON AT THE UNIVERSITY OF CHICAGO: THE EARLY YEARS

Although the University of Chicago played a leading role in the early training of Black sociologists, there was no tenured Black faculty in the department of sociology through 1970. On occasions, Black sociologists taught as visiting professors. The interdisciplinary academic community of the Chicago School was partly represented by Black scholars such as Allison Davis and Edgar Epps in education, John Hope Franklin in history, Eddie Williams in public affairs, and Walter Walker in social welfare. St. Clair Drake, a social anthropologist, taught at Roosevelt University. The national visibility of these Black scholars, alongside many others trained at Chicago, symbolized a legacy of leadership in scholarship and service. The Black presence at the Chicago School was partly maintained through Black graduate students and summer research and training programs that brought Black undergraduates to the campus. The "visible invisibility" of Blacks at Chicago was partly symbolized by a photograph of E. Franklin Frazier among other eminent Chicago School sociologists on the wall of the sociology department office.

Wilson initially came aboard at Chicago as a visiting associate professor and scholar in residence (1971–72) and became an associate professor in 1972–73. He indicates that upon his appointment and arrival at the University of Chicago, which coincided with the beginning of affirmative action, he was not universally received initially (Abramowitz 1991; Reynolds 1991). At this time, he remembers some "perceived misgivings" among colleagues upon his appointment at Chicago; they were suspicious of the abilities of Black professionals (Reynolds 1991). There can be little doubt that Wilson's presence and spirit as a professor challenged a history of unquestioned assumptions of White privilege, gentlemen's agreements that Blacks should be "outsiders," and discrimination in the department. The "perceived misgivings" episode appears to have been redefined by Wilson as a challenge that motivated him notonly to work harder but also to implement his iltellectual capacity. He states further: "I was determined to prove that I was not only capable but that I was better than the other scholars there" (Reynolds 1992). In another episode, he was appointed by the chair of the department of sociology as an associate editor of *The American Journal of Sociology* soon after his appointment he was challenged by another professor who was then editor with the query, "Can Wilson read?" (Remnick 1996, 101). This challenge further motivated him.

The early 1970s were a time when the Chicago School reestablished its leadership in the scholarship and training of Black sociologists. It is also noteworthy that the University of Chicago cosponsored a National Conference on Black Sociologists in 1972 which was designed to facilitate discussion and assessment of the contributions by Black sociologists to sociology (Blackwell and Janowitz 1974, vii–ix). This conference grew out of the cooperation between the caucus of Black sociologists and the American Sociological Association (Blackwell and Janowitz 1974, vii).

Wilson made an important contribution to the publication based on this conference with his theoretical essay, "The New Black Sociology: Reflections on the 'Insiders and Outsiders' Controversy." In this essay, Wilson made a unique critical appraisal of the Black approaches to race relations in terms of unresolved contradictions in the logic of scientific inquiry and professional objectives (Wilson 1974). Here he cautions against the excesses of what he calls the "Black solidarity" in the social science canons of the Black sociology of the 1970s. The arguments of Black sociologists' for a distinctive Black perspective in the sociology of race are critically examined (Wilson 1973). Taking issue with the "Insiders" doctrine "that individuals of a particular race or ethnic group have a greater intellectual understanding of a group's experiences," he emphasizes that there are no fundamental theoretical differences between the sociology of Whites and the sociology of Blacks. Furthermore, he underscores that a coherent and integrated body of thought in the new Black sociology does not exist (Wilson 1973, 325). He viewed the literature of Black sociologists on Black sociology as more polemical than scholarly.